Made with love for

....

by

....

This book is designed to inspire you to write about your memories following the guided prompts. Some questions may be difficult to answer or even not applicable, that's fine; you can change the questions to suit your circumstances or write about why you find them difficult. You can also draw, sketch, doodle or stick pictures into the pages to bring your memories to life. Above all, have fun filling in this book and give it to your child, so they can treasure your memories too.

Please visit happybearbooks.com for more beautiful books, news and freebies

Can you tell me about the time and place you were born? What's the story?

What are your earliest memories growing up?

Can you tell me about your mother's family?

Can you tell me about your father's family?

What interesting stories do you know about other people in your family?

Where did you live as a child? What do you remember the most?

What were your favourite childhood toys or games?

What pets did you have? What were their names? Would you have liked more pets?

Did you have holidays as a child and what do you remember about them?

Tell me about your friends when you were a child. Who was your best friend?

What was your school called? And what teachers did you like best?

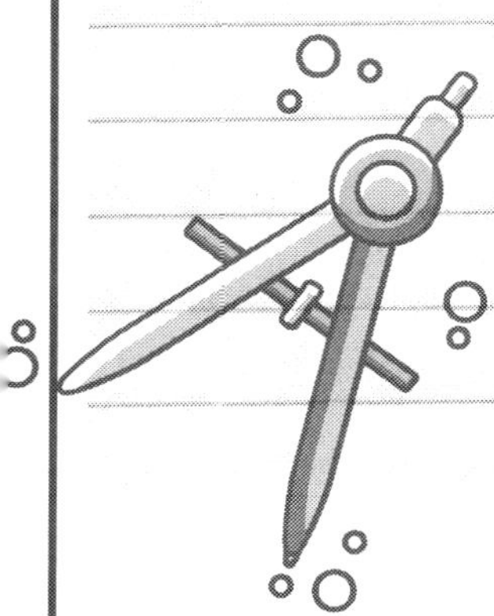

What were you good at ? What subject was your favourite at school?

Tell me an interesting or funny story about your childhood.

What did you want to be when you grew up?

What song or music did you like as a child? What was your favourite song?

Tell me about any books you liked to read or films or TV shows you used to watch.

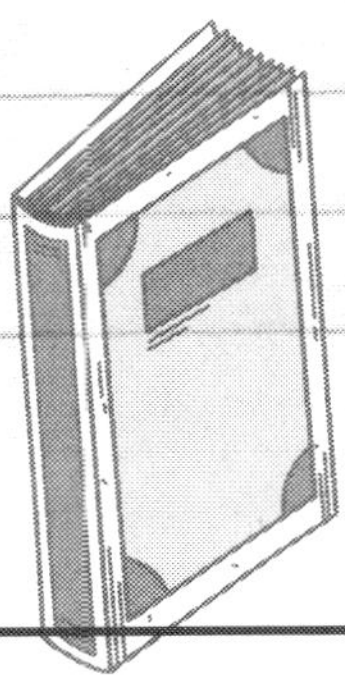

How do you remember your teenage years?

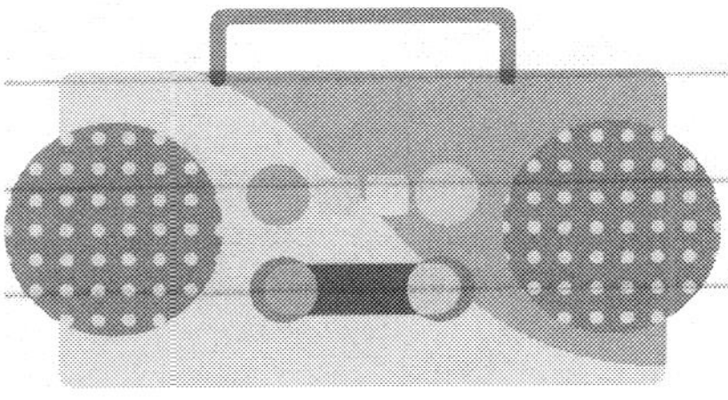

What music did you listen to and what films do you remember as a teenager?

Did you ever have your heart broken?

What was your first job?

What do you wish you had done then that you didn't do?

Did you still have the same childhood friends growing up? Did you make new friends as a young adult?

What did you get in trouble for as a child? What were you praised for?

How did you meet Grandma?

What has been your favourite saying or quote?

What do you think about being a parent?

Can you name a few of your favourite things ?
For example, favourite food, sport, colour...

Do you have any regrets? Why or why not?

What advice were you given by your parents?

What advice would you give me?

What was the best day in your life so far?

The rest of the book is for any stories that you may want to tell and memories that you would like to share.
You can also doodle or sketch anything that you feel is adding to your story.
Or maybe you would prefer to stick photos or images into these pages.
Above all, have fun!

To the World
You are a Grandad.

To our Family
you are the
World

A Grandad has silver
in his hair

And Gold

in his

Heart

Best Grandad

Printed in Great Britain
by Amazon

62833922R00061